THE SAHARA
AND ITS PEOPLE

Simon Scoones

Wayland

PEOPLE
· AND PLACES ·

The Amazon Rainforest and its People

The Arctic and its People

The Prairies and their People

The Sahara and its People

First published in 1993 by Wayland (Publishers) Ltd
61 Western Road, Hove, East Sussex, BN3 1JD, England

British Library Cataloguing in Publication Data
Scoones, Simon
  Sahara.—(People & Places Series)
  I. Title   II. Series
  966.03

ISBN 0 7502 0485 0

Typeset by Dorchester Typesetting Group Ltd
Printed and bound in Italy by G Canale & C.S.p.A.

Series Editor: Cally Chambers
Designer: Mark Whitchurch

Consultant: Dr Tony Binns is a geography lecturer in the School of
African and Asian Studies at the University of Sussex and
geography tutor for the university's teacher training course.

Cover: Nomads and their camels travel between oases of the Sahara in Algeria. They trade in all sorts of goods, including scarce firewood.

Title page: Women in Yatenga Province, Burkina Faso, have to walk for an hour to an area where they can find wood.

Contents page: Camels drinking at a waterhole in Sudan. Water is a limited resource in the Sahara.

Acknowledgements

The author would like to thank the following for their contributions to this book: The International Institute for Environment and Development, and Alison Brownlie at Oxfam Education, Brighton.

The publishers would like to thank the following for allowing their photographs to be reproduced in this book: Bruce Coleman Ltd. cover 4 (Ziesler),8 left (Sauer),8 right (Van Wormer),15 (Houston),24 & 31 (Henneghien); Robert Estall 10 (Beckwith); Explorer 5 inset (Guiter),7 main (Wolf),9 top (Thomas),9 bottom (Fouque),11 (Perier),13 (Amellar),14 top (Philippart De Foy),20 (Boutin),32 (Guiter); Jeremy Hartley 40 main; Hutchison 22,29,35 bottom, 38 & 44 (Errington),43; ICCE contents page; Christine Osborne 6,7 inset,17,28,33; Edward Parker 21,37; Science Photo Library 26 & 35 top (NASA); Still Pictures title page, 14 bottom, 16,27,36,41,42 (Edwards),30 (Wright); Tony Stone Worldwide 5 main; Tropix 19 both (Porter), 40 inset & 45 inset (Davis).
Artwork by Peter Bull (4,12 bottom, 24,25,26,28,32,35) and Peter Dennis (8,12,18,23,34,39).

CONTENTS

*D*eserts are one of the harshest kinds of environment on earth. Of all the deserts in the world, the Sahara is the biggest. Covering an area the size of the USA, it stretches about 5000 km right across Africa from the Atlantic Ocean in the west to the Red Sea in the east. The Sahara is so large that eleven countries lie partly or completely within it. But there is little life to be found in the Saharan desert itself.

Instead, it is in a belt of land along the southern edge of the Sahara that most of the life is to be found. This region is known as the Sahel. No border separates the Sahel and the Sahara – the two regions simply blend into each other. Travelling south from the Sahara, you would notice the trees and shrubs becoming more plentiful. The small groups of huts that make up villages would appear more often. Perhaps you would come

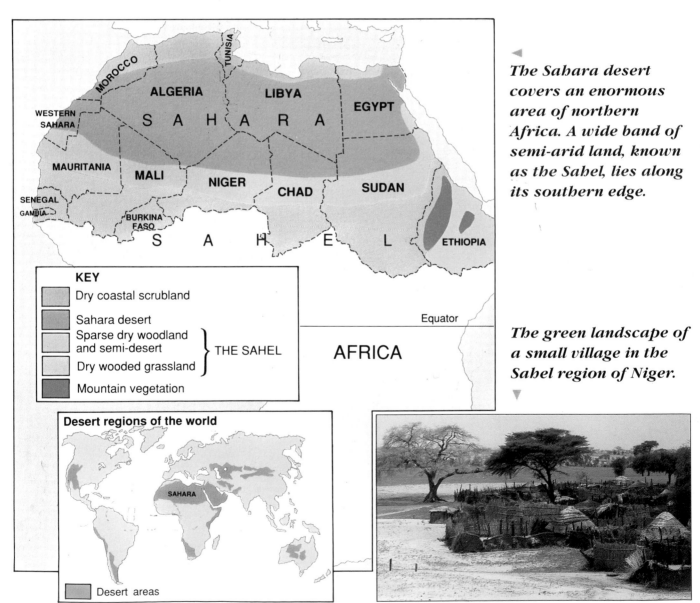

KEY

	Dry coastal scrubland
	Sahara desert
	Sparse dry woodland and semi-desert
	Dry wooded grassland
	Mountain vegetation

THE SAHEL

The Sahara desert covers an enormous area of northern Africa. A wide band of semi-arid land, known as the Sahel, lies along its southern edge.

The green landscape of a small village in the Sahel region of Niger.

Desert regions of the world

Desert areas

The Sahara is a place of contrasting landscapes. In Algeria, right in the heart of the desert, the scenery of dramatic sand dunes changes to steep mountains and wide plains.

across herds of goats grazing on the prickly vegetation and villagers here and there collecting firewood or tending their crops. This region, unlike the desert itself, is semi-arid and the little rainfall it receives each year is just enough to support plants, animals and people. There is life to the north of the Sahara too. The narrow strip of land along the Mediterranean coast is quite populated and busy with ports and towns.

People usually imagine the Sahara to be a vast area of golden sand dunes. In fact, the largest part of the desert is not nearly so spectacular and is covered by barren, gravel plains called regs. There are mountains too, some of them rising as high as 3500 m. Many of the rocks and stones on the regs are made up of old pieces of lava which once poured out of volcanoes in the area. The sweeping dunes are made when wind blows sand around large rocks and the sand collects behind them. A strong wind can easily shift the loose sand and change the shape of the landscape.

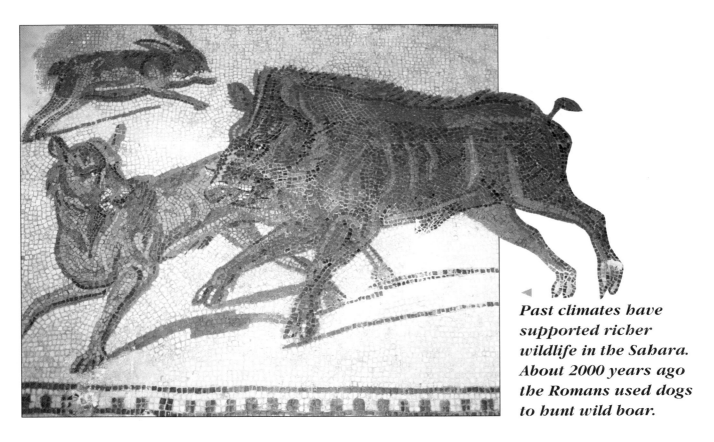

Past climates have supported richer wildlife in the Sahara. About 2000 years ago the Romans used dogs to hunt wild boar.

Cave paintings that are about 5000 years old have been found in the desert. They show pictures of people hunting big game animals. This gives us some idea of what the Sahara used to be like. Nowadays, it is too hot and dry for any of these animals to survive. Temperatures during the day rise above 45°C, and the ground surface can be too hot to touch. The desert gets hotter towards the Equator as the sun beats down directly overhead. The highest temperature ever recorded in the desert was at Azizia in Libya, where it reached 58°C in the shade. However, after the sun has set, the heat of the day quickly escapes into the clear night sky. There are not enough clouds to act as blankets to trap in the heat so it turns very cold. It is particularly cold between November and February, when the chilly and dusty harmattan wind blows in from the north-east.

People in the desert have learned to live with the extreme temperatures. They also have to live with the uncertainty of when the rains will come, if at all. Kharga in the Egyptian Sahara, went without a proper downpour for seventeen years. The rainfall in the region has always been unpredictable, but over the last twenty years there have been more and more periods of drought. No-one really knows the cause of this decline in rainfall. It could simply be the beginning of a drier period, lasting thousands of years, as part of a natural cycle in the world's climate. Or it could be a result of world climate changes brought about by the modern lifestyles of people.

READY TO SURVIVE

With such a hostile environment it is hard to believe that there is any life at all in the Sahara. But people, plants and animals have managed to adapt the way they live in order to survive. These adaptations may have taken thousands of years to evolve, or come about.

Water is rare and precious in the desert. Only plants that can obtain and hold on to the little water available can survive. Many plants, like the tamarisk bush, have incredibly long webs of roots that dig deep down to catch any moisture in the sand and rocks below. Others have a net of roots that spread out just under the surface. These catch any water that seeps into the ground as soon as it has rained. Plants often have thick waxy skins to stop water escaping from them.

Some cactus-like plants have also evolved thin spines which lose less water than large leaves. Many desert plants are adapted to poor, shallow soils and some can continue to grow in the high levels of salt that are often drawn to the surface of desert soils.

The seeds of plants need to be suited to the desert environment too. Many of them remain dormant in the sand, protected from the heat by their tough outer shells, until the rains come. Even after a short shower they soak up enough water to grow. In a matter of days, the desert can be transformed into a colourful bed of flowers. Such plants complete their whole life cycle within six to eight weeks. They can produce seeds for the next generation before the land dries up again.

▲
Many desert plants burst into life after a short rainstorm.

◄

The thick bark and waxy leaves on desert trees help them conserve water.

Acacia tree: Long thorns prevent grazing.

Date palm: Tough narrow leaves prevent water loss.

Camel: Hump stores water as fat.

Nostrils and long eyelashes keep out sand.

Special roots change nitrogen to nutrients in soil.

Skink: Tight jaws that keep out sand as they 'swim' through it.

Long roots reach down to water table.

Desert beetle: Waxy outer shell to keep heat out and moisture in.

Huge, flat feet that don't sink into sand.

Sand rat: Spends day in the cool safety of its burrow.

Fennec fox: Large ears help to locate prey at night.

Plants and animals in the desert are adapted to their surroundings, and exist in a delicate balance with each other.

The animals of the Sahara rely on the desert plants for their own survival. There are relatively few plants adapted to desert conditions and so there are fewer kinds of animals than can be found in wetter regions of the world. The climate of scorching days and sharp, cold nights determines how the animals behave. During the heat of the day, most animals hide underground in burrows, where it is both cool and damp. Most of the Sahara's animals are better suited to looking for food at night, but even they will seek protection in their burrows from the coldest hours before dawn. Fennec foxes leave their burrows to hunt for beetles and rodents as soon as the sun sets. The bodies of these creatures contain water that the fox needs. Because of the dark, fennec foxes rely on their hearing rather than their sight. They have especially large ears that can pick up sounds in the still of night to help them stalk their prey. These ears also help to keep them cool during the day when heat is easily lost through their large surface area.

A desert lizard sunbathes while keeping an eye out for tasty insects.

Scorpions have a tough skin to cut water loss, and a vicious sting to defend themselves and kill their prey.

Reptiles are cold-blooded animals and so need some heat to keep them active. They come out from shaded spots throughout the day to soak up the sun's warmth. Yet even reptiles need some shelter. Desert lizards and snakes can die within a few minutes if they stay out on the hot sand without shade.

As well as behaving to suit the climate, the creatures of the desert are adapted to food supplies available. Plants make their own food by using energy absorbed from sunlight. Some animals feed on the plants to survive. These herbivores in turn are a food source for meat-eating animals, and these animals may themselves be eaten by other carnivores. In this way, all living things are linked together in a food web. If one kind of plant or animal dies out, then the food supply of another creature is lost and its survival may be threatened. One simple change can have a knock-on effect to many living things in the food web.

It is not only the food web that is in delicate balance in the desert. The whole of the natural environment is fragile too. Although the environment can respond to changes, this usually happens over many thousands, if not

millions of years. In the Sahel, changes due to lack of rain and the actions of people are happening too quickly for the natural environment to adjust to them. More and more people use the land for growing crops and grazing animals. Wood is gathered for fuel and trees are being destroyed faster than they are replaced. As a result of such changes the environment is suffering from poorer soils and disappearing vegetation. Eventually areas of the Sahel could change permanently and become part of the Sahara desert.

·TRADING·ACROSS· ·THE·DESERT·

*L*ife in the Sahara desert has always been about survival. The two million people who live there come from generations that have been skilled in adapting to their surroundings. They have come to understand the difficulties of the environment and know how to make maximum use of the few resources they have.

The Tuareg is one of the largest groups of nomadic people, well adapted to the challenges of the desert.

The nomads of Niger use their skills as camel riders to herd their animals.

The Tuareg are a tall, proud desert people who have lived off their herds of animals for generations. They are nicknamed 'the veiled ones' because they cover their faces with cloth to protect them from the heat and dust. In order to survive they are nomadic, which means that they travel across the desert. They search out new grazing land for their camels and goats, and take care to move on to new pastures to give the vegetation a chance to recover. During one year, herds may travel about 1600 km in search of fresh pasture. This kind of nomadic grazing needs a large area because it produces only a small amount of food. Although the area is vast, it can only support a small number of people.

The animals are the most valuable possession of the Tuareg, but they often grow crops too and rely on collecting wild foods to vary their diet. Camels are especially important to the Tuareg. Their dung makes a good natural fertilizer for the poor desert soils and it can also be burnt as fuel. The camels are used for carrying goods across the desert. They also provide milk which helps to keep the people healthy. The size of a Tuareg's herd is a sign of wealth. A family with a big herd will be treated with respect by other families. Instead of using money, the Tuareg trade their animals in exchange for other goods.

Algiers, Tripoli, Tunis, Mogador, Fez.

Thieves would often lie in wait.

Salt, European weapons, copper and cloth.

Towering sand dunes had to be climbed.

The hot Harmattan wind blew fierce sandstorms.

Food and water had to be carried between oases.

Extreme temperatures above 40°C in the day and below freezing at night.

Slaves died along the way.

The track was dusty and stony. Often there was no track to follow at all.

Slaves, gold, ostrich feathers, ivory, leather and kola nuts.

Timbuktu, Kano, Kukawa

▲
Transporting goods across the desert was a risky business.

▶
Trade routes and oases still weave a pattern across the desert.

In the past, many groups of nomads traded by transporting goods across the desert, using their camels to form caravans, or convoys. Without the nomadic caravan traders of the desert, people living north of the Sahara would never have seen the gold, the great ivory tusks of elephants or the ostrich feathers which became very fashionable amongst European women. The nomads would sell these goods at high prices in the markets of Tripoli and other towns. For the return journey south they would load up their camels with the treasures of the north. Salt for example, was worth as much as gold in the southern markets of Timbuktu and Kano in those days.

Transporting slaves across the desert made up a large part of trade for people like the Tuareg. Slaves were in great demand in north Africa and Europe. They were forced to march barefoot for hundreds of kilometres. Travellers who followed the Saharan trade routes said that it was not unusual to see the skeletons of those who didn't make it.

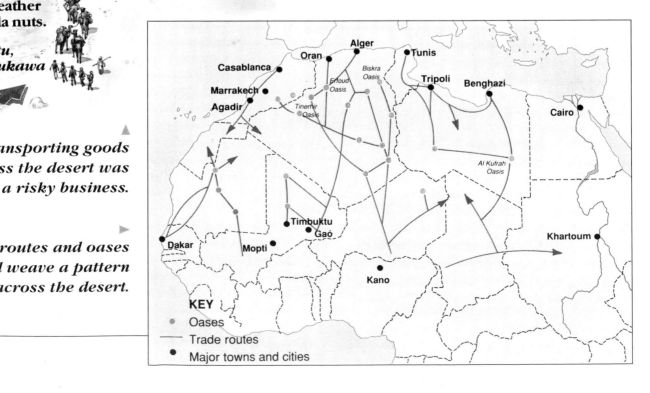

KEY
- Oases
- Trade routes
- Major towns and cities

STOPPING AT THE OASIS

Journeys across the Sahara could take about two months. Nomads had to be tough to cope with the hazards that they might meet on the way. To divide up the journey, find fresh supplies and rest, the nomads would often stop off at the oases which can still be found in the heart of the Sahara. An oasis is an island of life set in the expanse of bare desert where water springs up naturally from the ground. Here, people have built clusters of mud-brick houses around fields and gardens of date palms, tobacco and other crops.

Oases were commonly used as market places as well as stopping points. Oasis dwellers could trade their crops for the animals and other goods brought by the nomads. Nomads would sometimes act as the gangsters of the desert. They were paid protection money for promising safe passage to travellers between oases.

Life for the caravan traders and oasis dwellers was turned upside-down when the Europeans came to settle in Africa in the late nineteenth century. In time they brought the

Irrigation transforms the desert into fertile farmland. The Tinerhir Oasis at the foot of the Atlas mountains in Morocco is surrounded by date palms and fields of crops.

technology to build roads. People could transport goods right through the heart of the desert much more easily and safely than on the back of a camel. The Europeans also created new borders between countries, which made movement for the nomads more difficult. At the same time new trade routes were opening up in many other parts of the world and some of the traditional Saharan goods, such as salt, lost their value.

Today, nomads like the Tuareg still trade salt for food in the oases but the glory days of the caravan trade routes are gone. Instead, the Tuareg now earn extra money from making cloth and blankets from their animals. The women spin and dye the cloth which the men weave into beautiful patterns.

A Tuareg woman adds the finishing touches to a piece of cloth to be sold at Timbuktu market in Mali.

Many small oases, such as this one in Sudan, still exist in the desert. Farmers use traditional methods to irrigate their crops.

Modern irrigation systems like this one at Erfoud Oasis in Morocco, can channel millions of litres from underground water reserves.

DRILLING FOR WATER

More recently it has been discovered that by drilling below the desert, water can be found in more places than just the traditional oases. As a result, the richer countries of the Sahara have managed to make oases artificially. At the Al Kufra oasis in Libya, pumps have been used to get the water out of the rock below to irrigate a huge area of wheat. Today some oases have enough water to support large numbers of people. They are no longer simply stopping points in the desert. As many as twenty thousand people live at the Biskra oasis in Algeria. Dates are the main crop, many of which are sold abroad. It is mostly the women who tend the date palms and farm vegetable gardens of aubergines, carrots and onions, while some of the men have moved to northern cities to look for jobs with higher pay.

Irrigating crops on a large scale uses up a lot of water. Although there are large natural reserves beneath the desert, at many of the modern oases the water is being pumped out faster than it can be replaced naturally in the rock below. The water table – the level of water in the ground – falls. Life on the surface is threatened. At some oases, land is becoming drier and the date palms have begun to wither as their roots can no longer reach the falling water level. Farming crops becomes more and more difficult.

· CASHING·IN·ON· THE · LAND ·

*T*he main aim of a traditional farmer in the Sahara is to make sure that all the family members are fed enough to keep them healthy. Any extra food that can be sold at the market is a bonus. Many farmers use their crops or animals as currency; their way of life has little need for notes and coins. Farmers who live in this way are called subsistence farmers. It is often a different story in the Sahel where many farmers now grow crops, not to eat themselves but to sell at the market for cash. These cash crops are usually sold on to other countries. Things like the peanut butter you spread on your bread and the cotton shorts you like to wear in summer may all have come from such cash crops.

The work of children is important in threshing the peanuts to separate them from the bushes.

At the Kalsaka village market, Burkina Faso, women farmers sell their surplus produce. The money buys goods that they cannot make or grow themselves.

PEANUTS FOR CASH

Peanuts, or groundnuts, are the most important cash crop in Senegal and Niger, along the southern edge of the Sahara. About 200 years ago, peanut seeds were brought over from Brazil to Senegal. The French, who then ruled Senegal, did their best to encourage farmers to grow peanuts because they could not be grown in the French climate. The French needed more cooking oil which can be made from ground peanuts. They improved transport so that the harvested peanuts could be taken to ports from where they could be shipped abroad. New taxes, combined with the appeal of earning money, put pressure on subsistence farmers to give up their traditional way of life and grow cash crops instead.

Growing peanuts became a way of earning money for countries like Senegal and

Niger. They spent the money on goods from abroad which they could not make themselves. Unlike the widespread grazing of the land by the nomads, peanut farming was very intensive and could produce large amounts of the crop from each unit of land. Even today, when the people of Senegal and Niger rule their countries themselves, peanuts remain their biggest export. Many trees have been cut down to make way for huge peanut plantations, often on the best land.

At first, growing peanuts on the edge of the Sahara seemed like a good idea. They grew well in sandy soils and needed the long, dry periods to ripen. However, peanuts also need about 500 mm of rain each year and the unreliable rainfall of the region causes problems. In places the peanuts do not get enough rain to grow properly and in some parts of Senegal there is too much rain. Some of the areas cleared of vegetation have clay soils which hold water and leave the peanuts waterlogged.

After three years of growing peanuts, the land needs six years to rest and recover. This is called the fallow period. But with more and more peanuts being grown to earn money, farmers have been tempted not to leave the land fallow for long enough. As a result the soil loses its nutrients and the peanuts do not grow so well. The vegetation cover becomes poor and land is exposed to the winds that sweep across Senegal. Fertilizers have been used to replace the lost nutrients in the soil but they can make it crumbly and even more easily eroded. They are also very expensive and need to be used in larger and larger quantities as the soil becomes worse. Land that is misused in this way, suffers environmental damage that is hard to undo and the threat of the desert taking over increases.

It is not just the land that is suffering because of peanut cultivation. Nomadic farmers, who for generations have moved south to the edge of the desert to graze their animals, began to discover that a lot of the best land was being fenced off for peanut growing. They have been forced to return north and graze on poorer land which would otherwise be left fallow. Again, the soils suffer from over-use.

NO WAY OUT

Today, Senegal and Niger depend on the money raised from the sale of peanuts. However, the price of peanuts has fallen steadily on the world market while the price of manufactured goods, such as farm machinery, has risen. Farmers now have to produce more and more peanuts just to buy the same amount of manufactured goods from abroad.

In spite of the damage to the environment, the problems for the nomads and falling peanut prices, people continue to cut down

1980

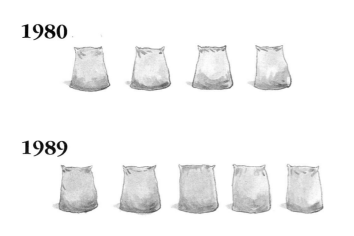

1989

Peanuts were worth 22 per cent less in 1989 than they were in 1980. Farmers have to grow and sell more peanuts just to buy the same number of manufactured goods.

Many countries cannot afford expensive foreign machinery like this crop-spraying aeroplane. ▶

In Libya, juniper forest has been cleared to make way for farming. ▼

trees to grow more peanuts, even when the land is unsuitable. In 1991, 45 000 hectares of forest in Senegal were cleared to grow peanuts, and 6000 nomadic farmers were forced off the land. Meanwhile, in other parts of Senegal, the soil has been worn out by peanut cultivation. It can no longer grow anything. Areas that used to be covered by rich soils and trees have been taken over by sand dunes.

You may wonder why Senegal and Niger don't start up other industries so that they would not have to rely so heavily on selling peanuts. In reality, it is difficult for them to raise enough money to start them up and they can't afford the technology to compete on the world market with big foreign companies. In a way, they are caught in a trap in which they have no choice but to carry on growing peanuts.

THE PEOPLE GO HUNGRY

Perhaps most worrying of all, the more land that is used for peanuts, the less land there is available for crops and animals to feed people. In the 1960s, Senegal produced more food than it needed. Today, more peanuts are grown, while people go hungry and food has to be brought from abroad. Some people think that if only the land could be more heavily cultivated, there would be plenty of food. Others worry that the more intensively the land is farmed, the less able it will be to feed people in the future, because of environmental problems. Some farmers have had enough of growing peanuts. The money earned from peanuts was not enough to feed their families. They have returned to subsistence farming of food crops.

At the height of the famine in Sudan in 1984, cotton was still being harvested on land that could have grown food.

A similar situation has developed on the eastern edge of the Sahara in Sudan. Organizations like the World Bank fund some of the development projects in Sudan. They have encouraged farmers to grow more cotton instead of food crops, because it makes money. Cotton is a cash crop which has been grown in Sudan since the British ruled the country from the middle of the nineteenth century. It is usually only the rich farmers who can afford to spend money on the machinery and irrigation needed to produce a good cotton crop. Meanwhile, poorer farmers cannot afford the high costs. They run into debt and lose their land to money-lenders. Some have migrated to cities like Khartoum, the capital of Sudan, in search of a better life. Many are disappointed. It is difficult to find work or housing in the city.

In the late 1970s, Sudan was self-sufficient in food. Now the country has to import wheat from the USA because so much of the land is used for growing cotton. This puts the country in a difficult position. Not only are the people helpless in controlling world prices of wheat and cotton but also, if the cash crops fail in a drought, many Sudanese have no food stores of their own to fall back on.

·IS·THE·SAHARA·SPREADING?·

A third of the earth's land is arid or semi-arid with less than 600 mm of rain per year and is home to 600 million people. Without proper protection half of this area of land could turn into desert. Desertification, or the spread of a desert, is most likely to happen where there is already low rainfall and the land has been used badly for years to the point that it is beyond recovery. This is the case along the edge of the Sahara where the naturally thin vegetation gives little protection to the soils.

◄

The small village of Tirelli huddles on the edge of the Gondo Plain in southern Mali. Its people cultivate millet and other crops in an area that is already threatened by drought.

A farmer at an oasis in Kardofan Province, Sudan, shows off an experiment to protect the village from creeping sand. By fencing off areas and planting trees during the 1970s, vegetation has successfully protected the land.

THE CLIMATE IS CHANGING

The Sahara has had a long run of years with lower rainfall. When the rains fail three or four years in a row, the underground water stores become empty and there is drought. In Mali, Lake Fagubine used to be the biggest lake in West Africa, and was a lifeline for many people who lived on the edge of the desert. During the 1980s, the lake dried up to no more than a puddle, and 60 000 people have been forced to move south in search of better land.

Although climatologists agree that rainfall has decreased in the area, they cannot agree on the reasons why. Some people believe that it has happened as belts of warm, drier air have shifted naturally towards the southern edge of the Sahara. Others believe that the desert and its borders will become hotter and drier because of the greenhouse effect. As people around the world burn more and more fossil fuels like coal, gas and oil, increasing amounts of carbon dioxide are being released. Carbon dioxide is one of the main gases that trap the sun's heat around the earth. Normally this greenhouse effect keeps the earth at a constant temperature, but as the gases build up in the atmosphere, the earth is becoming warmer and the world's climate patterns are thought to be changing. Whatever the cause, it is impossible to predict exactly how much rainfall the Sahara and Sahel will have in the future.

THREATENING THE LAND

It is likely that the region will remain at risk from over-cultivation in the future. Much of the best land has already been deforested to make way for cash-crop production like the peanut farming in Senegal and Niger. Often the cash crops are not suited to the conditions and need large amounts of fertilizers, chemicals and irrigation to make them grow. These can all threaten the quality of the land.

Good land does not turn into desert overnight. It is a gradual process that becomes harder and harder to stop. Plants, trees and shrubs growing on the land are the key to keeping it in a healthy balance. As soon as the vegetation is threatened, for whatever reason, the soil is at risk.

Plants Look After the Soil

Leaves provide shade and prevent soil drying to dust that is easily eroded.

Leaves form a kind of umbrella that stops rainstorms washing soil away.

Root systems of large plants and trees help bring underground water near the surface for smaller plants.

Young plants can grow up in the shade and protection of older plants.

Leaves and stems slow wind down and prevent it sweeping soil away.

Decaying plant material (humus) returns nutrients to the soil, improves soil texture, binds it together and holds on to moisture.

Networks of roots bind the soil together.

Some plants have special roots that convert nitrogen in the air to nitrates which are important for plant growth.

Plants do a lot for the soil. The humus, or fibrous organic matter, created when they die, gives nutrients back to the soil, binds it together and helps hold water in. It keeps the soil healthy and less likely to be blown away by the wind or washed away by a sudden rainstorm. The stems and leaves provide shelter for the soil too and their roots cling to it and prevent it from being eroded. The soil is kept damp and fertile and even more plants are encouraged to grow. The land flourishes.

As soon as plants are removed, eaten away or die off, the soil loses its protection. The sun dries and bakes the soil hard making it become fine and dusty. Once erosion has taken away the fertile topsoil, new plants find it difficult to grow and recovery is hard to bring about. Without action, the land slips into decline and may eventually turn into infertile desert.

The trampling and grazing of goat herds around Timbuktu, Mali, can only lead to further soil erosion.

Population growth adds to pressure on the land.

As large areas of the best land are taken up for cash crops, more people are forced on to poorer land. This land, particularly on the edge of the Sahara, is less able to support large numbers. Population growth here is often quite high. People are living longer and babies are surviving childhood diseases because of improvements in medicine. The contraceptives needed to control population growth are difficult to get or are too expensive for many people to buy. In fact, most people want lots of children in the hope that some will survive to work and produce food.

More people means more mouths to feed, so the land has to produce more food. Land that used to support traditional farming methods is farmed more intensively and land that used to be regarded as too poor has been brought into cultivation. The farmers are forced to ignore traditional farming methods that have developed in balance with the fragile environment. In time the land becomes even poorer in quality. As vegetation dies out the desert moves in.

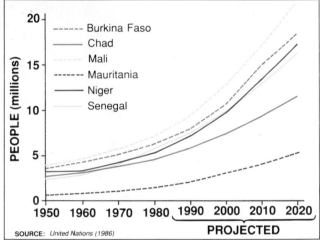

SOURCE: United Nations (1986)

PROJECTED

Where the nomadic farmers and their herds have been pushed off land to make way for plantations, they can no longer move freely and give the land time to recover from grazing by their animals. The nomads have gathered around wells where they can use the water and know that their herds will find good pasture. If the well becomes over-used, the water table in the ground below drops. The land dries out, the vegetation withers and dies and the soil is threatened with erosion. The animals can also do permanent damage to the surrounding vegetation by trampling and chewing young trees. Nomadic farmers do not deliberately damage the environment, but when they have been forced to graze in limited areas, soil erosion is more than likely to happen.

Most people in the Sahel rely on wood for fuel – as many as 90 per cent of Mauritanians use firewood. Many of the trees have already been chopped down and the land is being picked clean of its woody vegetation so that villagers have to walk further and further to gather wood. Such deforestation only increases the threat to the fragile environment.

The trees and crops that protect the soil are also under attack from a natural pest. Locusts have spread right across the Sahara. They like the hot temperatures and can breed very quickly. They lay their eggs in moist sand and in 10-20 days they hatch. Swarms of millions of locusts can even be spotted by satellite pictures as they are blown by the Saharan winds. One outbreak can devour a vast area of vegetation in minutes. Locust attacks were particularly bad in 1988. They destroyed half the crops in northern Burkina Faso. There is no easy way of getting rid of locust swarms. Chemicals can be sprayed from aeroplanes but they are expensive. The poisonous chemicals can also damage insects that are useful in controlling pests and diseases. They can even be passed along the food web and damage other animals as well as people.

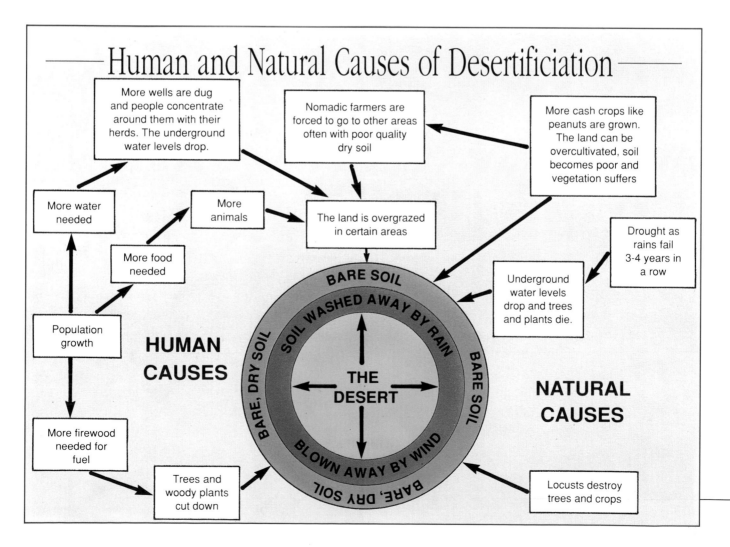

Human and Natural Causes of Desertificiation

More wells are dug and people concentrate around them with their herds. The underground water levels drop.

Nomadic farmers are forced to go to other areas often with poor quality dry soil

More cash crops like peanuts are grown. The land can be overcultivated, soil becomes poor and vegetation suffers

More water needed

More animals

The land is overgrazed in certain areas

Drought as rains fail 3-4 years in a row

More food needed

HUMAN CAUSES

Population growth

Underground water levels drop and trees and plants die.

BARE SOIL

SOIL WASHED AWAY BY RAIN

BARE, DRY SOIL

BARE SOIL

THE DESERT

NATURAL CAUSES

More firewood needed for fuel

BLOWN AWAY BY WIND

BARE, DRY SOIL

Trees and woody plants cut down

Locusts destroy trees and crops

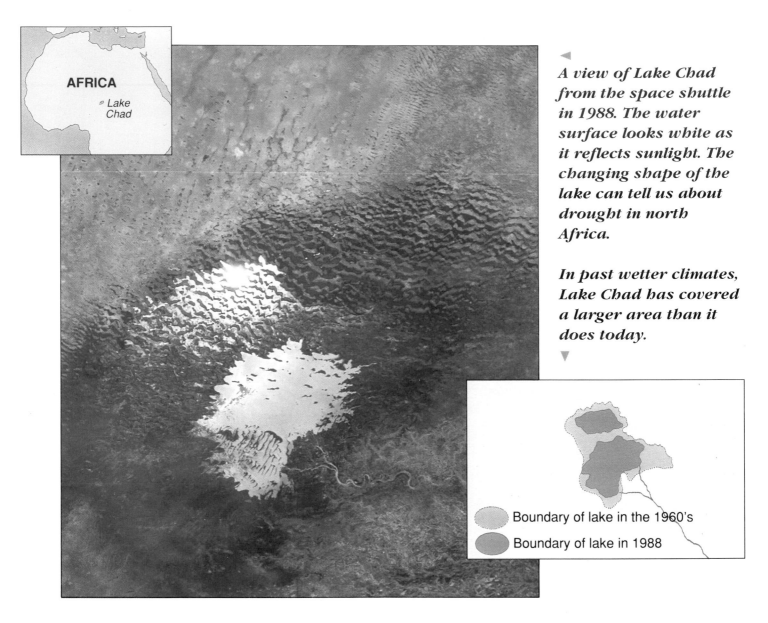

AFRICA

Lake Chad

◄

A view of Lake Chad from the space shuttle in 1988. The water surface looks white as it reflects sunlight. The changing shape of the lake can tell us about drought in north Africa.

In past wetter climates, Lake Chad has covered a larger area than it does today.

▼

Boundary of lake in the 1960's

Boundary of lake in 1988

The threat of the Sahara spreading southwards hangs over the Sahel. Some scientists used to believe that desertification had already permanently happened. They were relying on information from a few weather stations scattered across the desert. In the 1930s it was also thought that huge areas of the USA had turned into desert – some of those areas are now producing bumper harvests. More recently, satellite pictures taken of the Sahara show that the desert border changes from year to year. The desert in fact moves south and then back north again, getting bigger and smaller. There have been a few pockets of land that have been swallowed up by desert sand. But it will be a good forty years of research from satellite pictures before we will know for sure whether the desert is growing in a more permanent way.

· T R E A S U R E S · B E N E A T H · T H E · S U R F A C E ·

Gold fever has gripped people of Yatenga Province, Burkina Faso. Despite long hours of hard work, they find very little gold to make a living from.

Deserts often have many hidden treasures below their surface. Gold reserves have been mined in Western Australia, and copper has been dug out of the Kalahari and Atacama deserts. The Sahara also has plenty to offer. Underground, the Sahara is rich in minerals. By selling the minerals abroad, countries can make money with which they buy imports. Most of these minerals are dug up as ores.

These are the raw rock materials that contain bits of metal such as iron, copper, silver and gold.

Niger began mining uranium ore in the very remote, open plains of the desert south of Algeria. Uranium is a metal used in nuclear power-stations. When uranium atoms are split, huge amounts of heat are released which can be used for power. Uranium is made by melting down uranium ore. The ore is mined by the opencast method, in which layers of the desert are stripped off until rock is reached below.

Niger depends heavily on the money earned from uranium. Profits from uranium made up 75 per cent of all Niger's exports in 1989. However, like many other minerals, the price of uranium has fallen on the world market. This has meant that the average income of someone in Niger has dropped by 30 per cent, so there is less money to spend on the things people want to improve their lives. Countries like Niger would make more money if they could carry out mineral processing as well as mining. During processing

the metal is separated from the rest of the ore. But processing minerals needs technology which often only companies from richer countries can afford. In Niger uranium processing is run by a large French company.

Phosphorus is another mineral found in the Sahara. Western Sahara is the world's biggest phosphorus-producing region, making up about one third of the world's supply. An important phosphorus mine is located at Bou Craa in Western Sahara. Morocco also has deposits of phosphorus in the south. The mines at Khouribga and Youssoufia supply chemical works at Safi in the north. Here they use the phosphorus to make fertilizers, and phosphoric acid for use in industry.

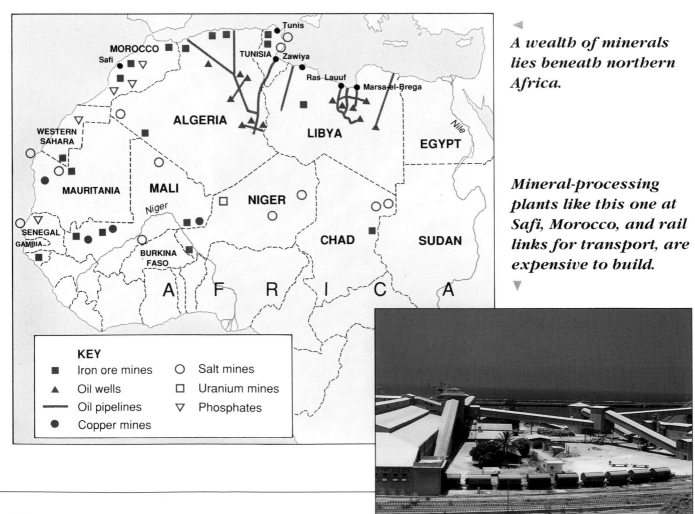

KEY

■ Iron ore mines	○ Salt mines
▲ Oil wells	□ Uranium mines
— Oil pipelines	▽ Phosphates
● Copper mines	

A wealth of minerals lies beneath northern Africa.

Mineral-processing plants like this one at Safi, Morocco, and rail links for transport, are expensive to build.

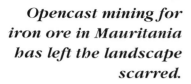

Opencast mining for iron ore in Mauritania has left the landscape scarred.

PROBLEMS FOR THE ENVIRONMENT

Very often, developing countries are so dependent on the income brought in from extracting and processing raw minerals, that they are unable to take the full costs to the environment into account. They have other priorities for spending their time and money, and pollution often goes on unchecked without being monitored or controlled.

Mining and processing minerals often upsets the environment. Mining can change the shape of the landscape. Huge amounts of rock are dug up, leaving gaping holes in the surface. It is also difficult to find a good use for the waste material which becomes piled up in enormous spoil heaps. In richer countries, spoil heaps are often flattened, then covered in soil and trees. But landscaping is

expensive for many Saharan countries. Instead, the environment is left permanently scarred.

During processing, the rocks are crushed. Dust is produced in large quantities and can choke plant life as the pores of leaves are blocked up. When iron and copper ores are processed, impurities are removed by smelting. The rocks are melted in a blast furnace and the metal is separated from the rest of the material. Poisonous gases, such as sulphur dioxide, are released and pollute the atmosphere.

Mineral processing also needs large quantities of water. In a region where water is already precious, the amounts of it taken for processing can only add to the problems of water shortage and falling water-table levels.

ROADS IN THE DESERT

The little water available in the Sahara is mostly used for irrigating crops or road building. Three cubic metres of water is needed to build every kilometre of road in the desert. Shortage of water means that roads across the desert sometimes fail to link up. Many roads are untarred and become impassable in the wet season. Even so, road building is seen as important in improving the transport of goods and minerals around the region. As much as two-thirds of foreign aid money in the southern Sahara was spent on building roads in the 1980s. A Trans-Saharan highway has been proposed that will follow some of the routes used by the nomads when they used to trade in salt and slaves. The road will be 3 500 km long, running from Algeria southwards across the desert to the ports in the west. More business will spring up along the road in the same way that it did at oases in the old days.

Despite the wealth of materials beneath the desert's surface, few Saharan countries have been able to develop industries beyond mining. Too often they lack the money and technical skills needed. Manufacturing industries need roads, railways, water and power in order to run factories, and few countries in the Sahara can provide these. Many countries, such as Mali and Niger, are completely surrounded by other countries and so do not have any ports on the coast. This makes it difficult for such countries to sell their minerals overseas. All these factors mean that manufacturing industries in and around the Sahara rarely employ more than a tiny proportion of the population. With the price of minerals continuing to fall, it seems unlikely that the situation will change.

The 'Uranium Road' in Niger provides an important route for transport and communications.

The discovery of oil in Saharan countries has brought great wealth to some people. But pollution from oil refineries, such as this one in Algeria, can harm the surrounding environment.

PRECIOUS OIL

Some Saharan countries have been more fortunate since oil has been discovered. Oil is a fossil fuel formed from living things which have slowly broken down over millions of years. Movements of the earth have made the oil collect in porous rocks like limestone and sandstone which are often sandwiched between layers of harder, impermeable rocks. Drills are used to make oil wells that reach the oil through the harder rocks. Some wells in Algeria are over 3 km deep.

Oil is carried by pipeline from the well to an oil refinery. Pipelines are expensive to build, especially if they stretch hundreds of kilometres across the desert. At the refinery, the crude oil is broken down into different types of oil. Oil refineries are usually on the coast because the processing needs large quantities of water. From the coast, it is easy to pipe the oil on to tankers which then transport the oil to other countries. Libya has set up refineries at Zawiya, Marsa-el-Brega and Ras Lanuf along its coast. However, there is always danger in oil drilling, refining and transportation. Explosions sometimes occur and spillages of oil can kill off wildlife and cause long-lasting damage to the environment.

It is difficult to find a substitute for oil as a fuel. Without it, the richer countries of the world would grind to a halt. This puts oil-producing countries in a powerful position. In 1962, Libya joined a group of countries which form the Organization of Petroleum Exporting Countries (OPEC). By clubbing together, the thirteen countries from all parts of the world can control the price of oil. In this way they can make sure they get a good deal on the world market.

Since the discovery of oil in Libya and Algeria, areas of the desert have been transformed from poor, dry farmland to busy industrial landscapes. Oil from Libyan and Algerian wells is high quality so it sells at a high price. Some of the money from the oil has been used to transform other parts of the desert into rich farmland. The products from oil refineries, such as the one at Das Lanuf, can be processed at petrochemical works for use as raw materials in industry.

· L A R G E · S C A L E ·
· P R O J E C T S ·

*T*here are many projects that have been set up to improve the lives of the people in the Sahara and the Sahel. Outside interest has come from organizations like the International Monetary Fund (IMF) and the World Bank. They use aid from the governments of richer countries to help developing countries. Charities like Oxfam and Action Aid also play an important role and work independently of governments. Overseas aid doesn't have to be in banknotes. It can be in machinery or technical skills. Sadly though, too much of this aid has not helped those who need it most.

In the past, the foreign aid donors have supported expensive development projects on a massive scale. These are similar to developments in richer countries like the USA, UK and Canada. The results can look good but they do not always suit the needs of the people or the environment.

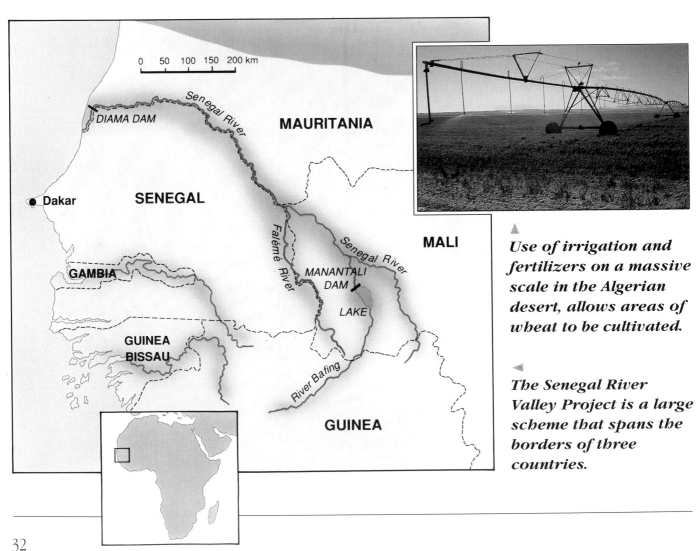

▲
Use of irrigation and fertilizers on a massive scale in the Algerian desert, allows areas of wheat to be cultivated.

◄
The Senegal River Valley Project is a large scheme that spans the borders of three countries.

THE SENEGAL RIVER VALLEY PROJECT

One such project can be found in the Senegal River Valley in the Sahel. This valley on the edge of the desert crosses the borders of three countries – Senegal, Mauritania and Mali. Although the valley is very dry, one million people live there. The people rely on the floods that occur during the short rainy season. When the Senegal River bursts its banks, nutrients are washed on to the land and improve the quality of the soil. But in some years, the rains have failed. The drought can ruin the fortunes of the people in the valley.

The governments of the three countries have worked together to form the Senegal Valley Development Organization. They are in charge of building two dams across the river which will be able to control the flow of water artificially. The water will be let out at regular intervals rather than relying on the natural floods. In doing so, the Senegal Valley Development Organization aims to irrigate a much larger area. With irrigation, six times more crops can be produced, as poor quality land is changed into productive farmland. At the same time, the dams can be used to generate hydroelectric power. This will provide more electricity for industry and people's homes.

Schemes like this are not cheap. It has cost $7 billion to build the dams at Diama and Manantali. More money is needed to maintain them in the future. There are also costs to the people of the area and the environment which can't be measured in terms of money.

Large areas of land previously used by local people had to be flooded as the water collected behind the dams. Ten thousand people have been forced to leave their

A region on the edge of the desert in Morocco flourishes. The dammed river produces hydroelectricity and irrigates a neat patchwork of fields.

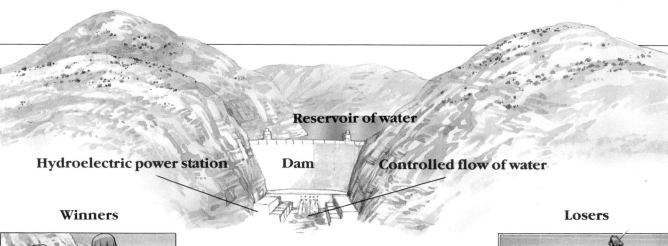

Reservoir of water

Hydroelectric power station   **Dam**   **Controlled flow of water**

Winners   **Losers**

 **Construction workers – often foreign companies.**   **Nomads who cannot use traditional grazing land.**

 **Electricity for factories and people in towns.**   **Small farmers who cannot afford irrigated land.**

 **Cash-crop farmers enjoy success on irrigated land.**   **Thousands of people who have to leave flooded homes.**

homes. Meanwhile the price of the improved land has rocketed as people compete against each other to buy it up. In south Mauritania, most of this precious land has been bought up by rich farmers. They have fenced off land to grow cash crops like cotton and rice. The traditional farmers like the Moors can't afford to buy the land and have had to move out. In the same way, the local nomadic farmers are blocked from using the valuable, irrigated pastures next to the river.

Now that the environment is flooded artificially, the dam operators need to be very careful about how much water is released. Too much water can waterlog the land. Too

little will leave the land parched and cause salts in the soil to build up. In both cases the risk of ruining the land is increased.

Local farmers in the valley used to plant crops after the rains had flooded the land, but now they can't work out when to plant them. In other parts of the valley, farmers have lost their supply of floodwater altogether. Because the flow has been redirected, water no longer reaches some areas. Without the floods, water table levels drop, wells dry out and vegetation dies away. Salts in the soil are no longer washed away by the floods. Instead, they build up and make the land poisonous to plants. All of these factors can

The Aswan Dam in Egypt has been successful in trebling crop yields. However, it has been widely criticized for some of the effects it has had on the environment.

River-damming schemes have winners and losers.

begin the familiar process of environmental damage that can lead to desertification.

Large-scale development schemes like the Senegal River Valley Project have winners and losers. But those who gain often don't live in the area. Improving the quality of the land is good news, but not for the local people who can no longer afford the high price of the land. Producing more electricity is a benefit to those who use it, but it is no good if the electricity is used up far away from the Senegal Valley, as is likely to happen. And of course, the more land taken up with growing cash crops, the less food is grown for the mouths of the people.

Bad drainage near El Kharga in central Egypt, has led to salts building up in the soil making farming impossible.

· S I M P L E ·
S O L U T I O N S ·

*L*ocal people can help a lot in improving the conditions in the Sahara and Sahel. After all, they know their environment well and have always adapted to making the most of limited resources. Very often, it is the locals who stand to lose most if large projects are not right for the area. They have every reason to make sure that small projects will help both them and their surroundings.

▲
Local farmers in Yatenga province, Burkina Faso, are keen to find out how stone lines can hold back water and soil, and improve the quality of the land.

In Dogon, Mali, women farmers are growing onions in shallow basins that hold in water.

On the Dogon Plateau in eastern Mali, the local people have developed their own ways of improving the environment. Here, they grow mostly millet and sorghum along with some peanuts and vegetables. But the soil is very thin and only a quarter of the land on the plateau is good enough for farming. Rainfall has declined in recent years so the people need to take care to conserve the limited soil and water. When they weed the fields, the weeds are left in piles next to the crops.

After a while, the dead plants mix in with soil to form mounds which act as mini compost heaps. These fertilize the land naturally as well as soaking up any rainfall before it can flow away, washing soil away with it. In places where there is deeper soil, the farmers dig shallow basins and pack earth around the edge of them. When the rains come or the land is irrigated, the basins catch every drop of water and form ideal garden plots in which to grow crops.

◄
Near the Red Sea Hills, Sudan, Oxfam have paid for concrete to make into blocks for building irrigation channels.

▶
There are many simple methods that will conserve the quality of the land. They rely both on old ideas and new techniques.

The important thing about these schemes is that they don't cost millions of dollars, nor do they rely on foreign machinery and technical skills. Organizations like Oxfam and Action Aid have been supporting the local people in the Sahel to develop these sort of home-grown improvement projects. Very often, the simple methods are adaptations of traditional ideas.

In the Yatenga province in northern Burkina Faso, Oxfam have given the people a supply of pickaxes and carts so they can collect rocks and stones to build low walls across the slopes of their land. The stone lines trap the water as it flows downhill so the valuable topsoil is not washed away. Instead, the water trickles out gradually through the small gaps between the stones. At the same time, bits of dead plant matter collect behind the walls to form a rich new bed of soil. It may be hard work building these stone lines, but the people of the Yatenga province have been very happy with the results. The year after the lines were completed, in 1984, crop yields nearly doubled.

Simple Solutions to Save the Soil

Growing crops mixed in with plants that fix nitrates in the soil.

Forming stone lines that hold back water and soil after rain.

Building hillside terraces to hold back soil and water.

Using weeds to make compost mounds.

Planting rows of trees to act as windbreaks and protect the soil from erosion.

Leaving vegetation to grow and protect the soil.

Using cooking stoves that burn less wood to save cutting down trees for fuel.

Digging shallow basins to hold rainwater back in vegetable plots and control irrigation water.

▲
Cowpea can be grown with millet to add nitrogen to the soil.

▶
In Burkina Faso, villagers get together to plant trees along a stone line.

The people of Yatenga have also planted a lot of trees. Trees can be a lifeline for the people and environment of the Sahara. They can act as a shady windbreak and stop the fertile topsoil drying out and blowing away in the strong winds that sweep across the desert. Meanwhile their roots bind the soil together and trees like the acacia fertilize the soil by adding nitrogen and phosphorus. Trees bring other benefits as well. If they are managed properly, some trees can produce fruit for people to eat. Others provide food for animals, as well as wood for fuel and for making building poles. These ideas, developed by the people of Yatenga, have been passed from village to village so other communities have also benefited.

Voluntary organizations can help the people to help themselves by providing them with cheap technology suited to local conditions. Supplies of basic, cheap machines and tools which can be repaired locally can enable farmers to use their land more efficiently. Seeds of trees and shrubs that can withstand the dry, hot conditions can be distributed. These protect the soil from erosion and provide food for farmers' animals. In Toudouf, western Algeria, War on Want gave the people a pump so they could obtain water from underground even though it is in the heart of the Sahara. The locals have used the water on a small scale to irrigate large vegetable gardens of carrots, beetroot, potatoes and water-melons.

The experiences of the Dogon Plateau, Yatenga and Toudouf all show what people can do to improve production from the land without spoiling it. However, one of the main obstacles to such development is that large amounts of land is often owned by only a few people. In the Senegal River Valley, the good quality irrigated land has been bought up by a handful of rich farmers and the government to grow cash crops. Farmers won't work as hard to improve the land if it is owned by somebody else or if they think that they might be forced to leave it. Perhaps if land was shared out more equally the Sahara would see more success stories. Distributing the land so that everyone has a share is called land reform. Nomadic farmers like the Tuareg would benefit a lot from land reform.

By letting them on to more land, they would not be forced to over-graze certain areas and the risk of desertification would fall.

The big aid-givers like the World Bank are beginning to learn that the key to success is in listening to the needs of local people, and involving them in decision making. A stone wall or a row of trees may not look as impressive as a huge dam project, but the results speak for themselves. However, it would be too simple to say that local people are better off without modern technology. Many of the methods developed by local people to improve the environment could benefit from technology if it were cheap and appropriate to local needs. Such local development projects could well solve many problems for the Sahara region in years to come.

A woman cooks over a simple stove designed by experts in Burkina Faso. It uses less firewood than a traditional fire (to the left of the picture) and therefore reduces the rate of deforestation.

Fleeing from war and drought, many people in Ethiopia have been forced to take to the road in search of a more secure life.

For children in Ethiopia, having an education means a better chance for the future.

The countries of the Sahara and Sahel face some major challenges in the future. Researchers of climatic change predict that temperatures could increase by between 1.5 °C and 4.5 °C over the next 60 years, and rainfall could continue to decline. The environment of the Sahel would change with the climate. Many plants and trees would die off and the natural balance of the environment would alter. Parts of the Sahel could become so badly affected that they change into desert.

If the Sahara did spread permanently south into the Sahel, the effects could be devastating for millions of people. In richer parts of the world that are threatened by desertification, such as areas of Australia and the western edge of the Prairies in the USA, people have the best chance of survival. For many people of the Sahel who lead a subsistence lifestyle, the spread of the desert is a life and death situation.

If more land turns into desert in the Sahel, it will produce less food. At the same time, population growth means that there will be more mouths to feed. The lives of 30 million people in the Sahel could be threatened with famine. The drought in 1990 in Chad, Sudan, Mauritania and Ethiopia made the risk of famine a real possibility. Although the rains came in 1991, drought has hit parts of Africa again in 1992.

Richer countries can buy the technology that can fight desertification. In southern Australia, imported plants and fertilizers are used to restore the land. In the Sahel, governments cannot afford these solutions. Governments and foreign aid can help, but there is no point in throwing money at the problems, hoping that they will disappear. Large-scale

projects like the Senegal River Valley development are not necessarily the answer. Pumping money into cash crops like peanuts will only continue to create problems for people and the environment.

HELPING THE PEOPLE TO HELP THEMSELVES

The Sahara and the Sahel are made up of different countries with many contrasts in the human and natural environments. Because of this, there is no single way of solving the problems of the region. Small, local-based developments are more likely to enjoy success. Local people do not feel that they need a completely new way of life imposed on them from outside. Instead, development of the region could build on the successes of local people in coping with the hostile environment. They should be involved in decisions about how to manage the land, using their skills and knowledge of their surroundings. In this way, local people would have greater control over their own future and be more able to conserve their environment.

Above all, the basic needs of people need to be met. The ordinary farmer wants to be able to provide shelter for his or her family and enough food to feed them. People therefore do not need to feel trapped into growing cash crops before food. At the same time, people need help in increasing food production without ruining the environment. They need help in finding alternatives to destroying trees for firewood. People in Mali and Mauritania have received cheap natural gas from Algeria as a source of fuel instead of firewood. With better health facilities, water supplies and education, people will be less at risk in times of drought.

Until recently, half the government budget in Ethiopia was spent on a civil war that has been raging for years.

Striking landscapes of the Sahara could encourage tourism as source of income. (Inset) Local people have a lot to offer towards the future.

MAKING THE SITUATION WORSE

Drought and environmental misuse are not the only factors that cause famine in the Sahara and Sahel. Conflicts between people bring a risk of famine too. Parts of the Sahara region have been torn apart by war. In 1975 Morocco invaded Western Sahara and there has been conflict in that region ever since. The money spent on arms to fight these wars is at the expense of improving the basic needs of the people. Conflicts such as these destroy any hope of building up industries and independence from foreign countries. Foreign aid received is difficult to transport through war zones and food may not reach people who need it. If there is to be peace in the future, co-operation needs to come from countries outside of the region too. Most of the weapons for war are supplied by the richer countries of the world.

The international community could also help with the Sahara's trading position on world markets. As a member of OPEC, Libya is paid a better price for its oil. But Saharan countries that depend on the sale of cash crops and minerals abroad have no power in controlling the prices for their goods. Prices for these products have fallen while manufactured goods which have to be imported have become more expensive. If fair agreements on pricing could be reached between countries, the people of the Sahara and Sahel would be in a better position to help themselves and their environment.

TOURISM – A NEW INDUSTRY?

In many developing countries, tourism has become a valuable source of wealth, although sometimes it has brought with it a new set of social and environmental problems. Resorts have developed along much of West Africa's coastline. Although the Sahara itself cannot offer seaside holidays, tourism could still be encouraged. The Paris to Dakar car rally, which crosses several Saharan countries, already brings many visitors to the region. At present, there aren't many facilities for tourists. But the stunning beauty of the desert with its vast sand dunes and impressive mountain ranges may attract more tourists in the future.

The future of the Sahara is unwritten. It very much depends on how attitudes of the outside world and governments in the region develop. If the Sahara is to have a secure future, some balance needs to be drawn up between the people and their environment. The importance of local communities in finding this balance is slowly being recognized. Perhaps we should look to them first for the way forward.

GLOSSARY

Cash crops Crops that are grown to sell as a main source of money.

Contraceptives Methods of preventing women becoming pregnant.

Crude oil Oil before it has been separated into different types of oil in a refinery.

Deforestation The clearance of trees from the land.

Desertification The spread of a desert because of both declining rainfall and the way the land is misused by people.

Development A term that describes the growth and change of farming, industry, the environment and people's lifestyles in the less industrialized countries of the world.

Erosion The wearing away of rock and soil by the movement of water, wind or animals. Once erosion of the land starts, it usually continues to get worse if nothing is done to correct it.

Exports Raw materials and products that are sold abroad.

Fallow period A time when no crops are grown to allow the soil to rest and become fertile again.

Famine An extreme shortage of food. Poorer people may starve or die because they cannot grow or buy enough food.

Fertilizer Nutrients added to the soil to keep it fertile and able to grow crops. Chemical fertilizers are made in factories and natural fertilizers come from animals and plants.

Foreign aid The food, money, materials or services given by richer countries to support developing countries.

Impermeable rock Rock that water cannot pass through.

Imports Raw materials and products that are bought in from abroad.

Intensive farming Farming that produces a lot of crop or feeds a large number of livestock for the area of land used.

Irrigation Methods of artificially watering the land to help crops grow.

Land reform The re-distribution of land more equally between people.

Manufactured Made in factories.

Migrate To move to another area or country.

Nomadic A way of life in which a people are continually on the move within a region.

Over-cultivation Farming the land so much that it becomes poor quality.

Plantation A large area of land that is used for growing crops, often cash crops.

Processing When raw materials are broken down and turned into substances that are useful for manufacturing.

Raw materials Basic substances that are used for manufacturing.

Semi-arid Dry land or climate, with an annual rainfall of about 25-60 cm.

Subsistence farming Producing crops and rearing animals with the aim of feeding the farmer's family. Any surplus is sold at market for extra income.

World Bank The popular name for the International Bank for Reconstruction and Development, set up especially to lend money to countries to encourage development.

· B O O K S T O R E A D ·

Desert Animals by Mark Cawardine
  (OUP 1987)
Deserts by Martyn Bramwell
  (Franklin Watts 1987)
Deserts (Animal Homes) by Robert Burton
  (Belitha Press 1991)
Deserts (Wild World of Animals) by Michael
  Chinery (Kingfisher 1991)
Let's Go to Ethiopia by Keith Lye
  (Franklin Watts 1986)
Let's Go to Morocco by Keith Lye
  (Franklin Watts 1988)

Let's Visit Burkina Faso by Aaron Lear
  (Chelsea House US 1986)
Let's Visit Libya by Renfield Sanders
  (Chelsea House US 1987)
Let's Visit Senegal by William Lutz
  (Chelsea House US 1989)
Life in the Deserts by Lucy Baker
  (Franklin Watts 1990)
Looking After Our Land by W Critchley
  (Oxfam/IIED 1991)
24 Hours in a Desert by Barrie Watts
  (Franklin Watts 1991)

· U S E F U L   A D D R E S S E S ·

Action Aid
Old Church House
Church Steps
Frome
Somerset BA11 1PL

Council for Environmental Education
School of Education
University of Reading
London Road
Reading RG1 5AQ

Friends of the Earth (Australia)
PO Box A474
Syndey
NSW 2001

Friends of the Earth (Canada)
251 Laurier Avenue
W Suite 701
Ottowa
Ontario K1P 5J6

Friends of the Earth (New Zealand)
PO Box 5599
Wellesley Street
Auckland West

Friends of the Earth (UK)
26-28 Underwood Street
London N1 7JQ

Oxfam
274 Banbury Road
Oxford OX2 7DZ

WWF UK (World Wide Fund for Nature)
Panda House
Weyside Park
Godalming
Surrey GU7 1XR

INDEX